Echoes

of a

Silent Battle

(POETRY IN MOTION)

MARIO RIOS

Dedication

*To my wife and kids-Your love has been my
anchor, your patience my refuge,
and your laughter my healing. Through the storms
you reminded me of what truly matters,
and in the silence, you gave me strength.
This book was born from battles I fought,
but it was your faith in me that carried me through.
Every page I have written
is marked by your presence, and every step
forward is because of you.*

Acknowledgement's

I want to acknowledge all those who walked with me through fire and faith-your prayers and presents were my life line.

To: My family and friends who encouraged me and celebrated with me in moments of victory.

To: Carlos Vigil, A brotherhood shared by few. I had that with you.

To: Andrew Sandoval, for showing me how to enjoy life to the full. Years pass, still—I miss you everyday.

To: My mission brothers, who reminded me that faith and service can transform hearts, including my own.

To: C, who's conversations taught me to believe in new beginnings.

To: My Pastor, for speaking truth into my life when I needed it most and for reminding me that God's grace is always greater than my failures.

Pen to Paper

Years of words, printed images of growth and pain,

But words left alone lose their meaning.

Far too long, confusion silenced my hand.

*I listened, what's next
shall be written.*

Today, I put pen to paper.

Not knowing what will be…

8/27/22

Introduction

"Echoes of a Silent Battle " is more than a collection of poems—it is a record of an invisible war.
Not a war with the world, but one within myself; one that can only be won by surrender.

For years, I wrestled with questions about, purpose, direction. Could I make a difference? What was I doing? Some days felt loud with noise, others deafening in silence. But in those moments of stillness, pain or pressure… something shifted.

Victory was not fighting harder. Victory was letting go.

These poems were written in the middle of that process; in notebooks, on quiet nights, during breakdowns, and breakthroughs. They are echoes of that silent battle. And if you are in one of your own, I hope they help you feel less alone.

"The explanation is in you!"

12/31/21

Backstory of
Echoes of a Silent Battle (Poem)

Chapter 1

For twenty years, I wrote in silence.
No one knew I kept a pencil moving.
No one knew my pages were full of battles, questions, and cries.

That old blue notebook carried worn pages—concealing pain, struggle, love, laughter, loss, and triumph . It stood the test of time, screaming to get seen!
I was a story etched in woven words.

Time stood still as I fell deep into its pages.
Perfection went unnoticed. The words became a conduit, flowing through my hand, grounding me to a fragile love story with life.

But the words were not fiction.
They mirrored my war.
A non-fiction story of a man living in sin.

I had been a prisoner long enough.
The silence grew loud.
The sound of battle drums called.
The war I never saw coming—an ambush of the enemy.

Kneeling in my backyard, I surrendered while my stepdad spoke words that changed my life.
The enemy put on notice, searching, but I could not be found—hidden by the pages of my Bible and a pencil in hand.

My armor is scarred, battled, and beaten.

Scratched its way to life.
My decision erupted an all-out war.

Tension I never knew I carried broke loose.
With loss came grief, which led to self-conviction.
My morals drowned. Doubt never let me rest.
I was tired of being tired.

The enemy had already devised his scheme.
I had no clue what was coming.

In a blink of an eye, my world was turned upside down.
The place I would find shelter when I needed to rest. Had been attacked. And my best friend of 25 years was taken. His silent battle had been waging war. Was I blind?

(Damage to my chest, my heart stopped beating.)

The enemy using this to invade, attacking my mind. Thinking I had failed, self doubt broke down the front lines.

I never feared he would fall. He was the strong one—the rock, the mortar holding everything together.

I said goodbye. "I love you, bro."
I drove away, not knowing it would be the last time I see him alive.

(Alone. Searching for the part of me that died that day.
I'm lost not defeated.)

Soon after, my marriage was under its own attack.
My children were distancing.
I tried to keep it together, attacked by
the veterans of fear.
I slipped back into familiar shadows.
Vulnerable. Hiding.

In the darkness of those shadows I lay sleeping.
And with my hands raised, I ask God to forgive me. What I thought was the end, had become my beginning.
A voice hit me like an earthquake-cracking my weak foundation.
Speaking to my soul, I heard…

"It's going to be okay."

The peace I felt was foreign to me. My soul was alive. And my mind was eased.

So forward I moved, inch by inch.
And when I took a step back. God's disciple was there. He reminded me that I was not alone. His words, "I will not give up on you, thats not what I do."

Words I hold close to this day. My battle song sounded for the the enemy. Gripping my sword tight.

The men of my church became examples—walking through their own battles with obedience, discipline, and surrender. They carried peace and stability, and I followed.

I studied until I understood why they could move forward. My walk became clear. And purpose was no longer a question.

(What will be done? Determined purpose, pay no mind to the question.)

And still, I wrote.
My pencil directing language, conducting a symphony.

The words were not just remnants of a broken man, but the testimony of surrender that had become victory.

I had been writing parables of life.
Each one telling *my story*.

Yet one poem still eluded its ending.
I added, erased, rewrote, every word written confusing the next.

It was stubborn. I would turn my back on this poem only to find it writing the script once more.

"Rest,
get back to living
And moving with reason.
Believing—you are the reason."

M.Rios

Stay strong in the moment

Stay strong in the moment.
Don't let the moment change your strength.

Moments of life can feel like a war fought alone.
The war can be won by the broken.
Broken will be fixed when you understand what tools it takes to rebuild.
War has no winners, just survivors.
The real war is fought after surrender.
Confusing words to the confused.
Strength that can only be gained by pain.
Destructive strength unless understood in depth.
Few understand and most fail.
To the few now is time to listen.
Nothing you speak will be heard.
Your words fall on deaf ears.
Language of pain is only earned wisdom of faith.
A silent award that is never recognized but all the often awarded.

To the strong belong the spoils, to the faithful belongs the victory, to the Holy belongs the Glory forever and ever.
Amen

"Pay attention now. The conversation has no battery. Your walk is not dictated by a time line. Rather by your decisions that dictate your time. The clock will continue long after your gone."

M. *Rios*

Chapter 2
Living With Open Hands.

I signed up to go on a mission to Cuba. with the men from my church. We each had to raise $2,400, and I saved what I could. My dad and step-mom gave me $400 at Christmas to put toward the trip.

A friend of mine asked if he could hire me to do some work at his house. It was not difficult, and I planned to do it for nothing — like friends do. But he insisted on paying me. He would not take no for an answer. So, I told him I would put it toward the Cuba trip. It was $600.

With two months left I still owed $1,200. dollars. Then, a couple of weeks later, that same friend was finishing up the second phase of his home project and asked for my help once more. And when I finished he told me that he and his wife wanted to pay off the remaining balance of the mission I was going on.

This act has impacted not only myself and countless others. But is proof that living with open hands has the power to change lives.

He had no idea what this meant to me. It was the three-year anniversary of my best friend's passing. All day I had been thinking of him. It was hard holding it in. Driving home as the tears fell down my face. I was humbled. This is one of my churches core values and I was the recipient of it.

Think twice

Life's clock set to expire.
Second hand turning desire.

Lost time with no future.
Future time with no past.

Compass for direction.
Unbeaten path.

Time much needed.
Needed much time.

Forward we move.
Lead by the blind.

Important can wait.
Impatient becomes fate.

Time has chosen time.

We all have a date.

Chapter 3

And Off to Cuba I Went.

We arrived on a Monday and toured the church we would work on. It was huge, unfinished, and in need of much labor. The next day we began our task: digging a hole. A septic tank was needed for the restrooms, and 44 tons of dirt — 88,000 pounds — had to be moved with picks, shovels, and wheelbarrows.

Watching Samson slay the tree we became unstoppable. Nobody complained. We just got it done. As I swung my pick into the earth, I realized I was digging out the old foundation of my life. With each strike, I tore away years of weakness. For four days I did not stop. By Friday, we had moved enough earth. The crowds came to see. Thankfully, Saturday would be a day to visit other churches.

Saturday morning began with guava, papaya, and coffee, as usual. And every morning, someone new shared a devotional. It was my turn. I had never given one before. I prepared all week, writing it out in the notes app on my phone — right alongside the unfinished poems I always carried.

During one of our rides back to the hotel, I shared a few of those poems with the men. To my surprise, their reaction was not embarrassment or judgment. They leaned in. Their encouragement gave me the ending to my devotional: I would close by sharing a poem.

But which one? Many were still torn apart in revisions — erased, rewritten, dissected endlessly, then put back the same way. Yes, It was frustrating. I could never seem to finish them. Especially the one that eluded me.

That Saturday morning, I was awakened early from a dream that would not let me sleep. So, I reviewed my devotional, satisfied with what I would say. I glanced at my notes — and there it was. My nemesis. The unfinished poem.

And for the first time, I could see the words fall in line. It was writing the ending. Reveling itself. I was distracted. Called to breakfast. That poem always had a way of changing the script.

After breakfast, I stood and shared my devotional. My message was for the men:

Do not stop teaching. We are still listening, even when it does not seem like it. Their influence had brought me this far. And this was my thank you, without saying the words. Their structure and discipline would not hear "thank you" anyways. Humble they walk.

When I finished, I still needed a closing. Prayer would have been the common choice. Instead, I read my poem.

I read it like I was back home, late at night, lost in the story. Living it. Breathing it. And when I reached the ending, the next sentence broke through:

"I" has became "We."

I looked up. Not a dry eye in the room. My words had pierced not only my story, but theirs. I saw their battles reflected back in their faces. My mind replaying the dream. I Knew what needed to be done.

As things calmed, someone said, "Happy Birthday." I had mentioned it months before to one of the leaders. He remembered.

It was my 40th birthday. Four years to the day since I wrote the first sentence after surrender. God's timing, once again.

I could not stop thinking of the dream that woke me? It was not just a dream. It was a familiar voice. The voice that once whispered, "It's going to be okay."

But this time, I heard:

"THIS ISN'T FOR YOU"

*"My silence is loud,
never to be heard.*

My silence is loud,
healing with words.

My silence is loud………"

M.Rios

Weathered Boots

Time will continue its lust for the future.
Relentless chase leaving without a trace.
Your boots don't recognize time.
They battle to hold it together,
As strength fades from leather.
Worn every season has made the soul stand uneven.

New boots have been waiting,
Your tread made for saving
Breakthrough the path as
you travel the past.
Forgive yourself.
This too shall "pass!"
The gift of new-
boots weather the time.
Made for you
so continue the climb.
You have been called to a
new place.
Your Weathered Boots have a
new pace.

"Our conversations had the strength to lift the weight off my heart.

Prayer is our conversation now, with the strength to never part"

M. Rios

Forged

*Righteous I've become words whispered by the flesh.
Gossip of the blind and weak.*

To be righteous isn't a title, but a way I seek.

*I bow my head, I bend my knee—His grace reborn
has set my soul free.*

*I've laid my sword down, but my grip still remains,
for in its steel, Jesus is engraved.
The battle was meant to be mine. I am not alone.*

Jesus gave his life, And the veil has been torn.

*Purchased with his blood, His robe wrapped around
me,*

"it is finished"

Truly majesty.

The finality of my story

I thank God—and all His Glory.

Chapter 4

Returning

Hugs tried to hold on. Gratitude poured out. We had come to serve, but by the end of the trip I could not help but feel we were the ones that had been served. The Holy Spirit was upon us all week.

The three-day journey home was filled with silence and thought. I replayed the moments, humbled by the generosity and kindness we were shown. How do you explain a feeling that has no words?

The poem still lingered in my mind. I realized this mission aligned with the very sentences I had written years earlier. I knew there was more.

Our leader on the trip was one of the men I had once watched from afar, back when my path had no direction. His advice was always solid. I trusted that if I placed a copy of my poem into his hands, he would know what to do with it. So, I slipped it into a folder I was holding for him. It was my way of obeying the words I had heard in my dream. My prayer was simple: Lord, let this reach the ears it needs to.

That is exactly what happened—only bigger than I would ever imagine.

A week before Easter, my pastor called. He asked if I would share how I came to Christ. They were preparing a montage of four testimonies to play during the Easter service. I knew this was my chance.

My pastor already had the poem—someone had shared it with him in a meeting, and it sat on his desk. I asked if I could read it live, not just on video. I explained why it mattered, and he agreed. He had been with me from the beginning of this journey, yet even he did not know the full backstory.

So, I shared my testimony on video like the others, and when the time came, my video played last. As it ended, the lights shined bright—and there I was, standing on stage. Poem in hand.

That moment was the final chapter of this long journey. It took everything in me not to break down. Years of words condensed into a couple of minutes. Words written in every season— frustration, triumph, grief, surrender. Words that refused to be finished until now.

After the service, people I knew and people I had never met approached me. Their words of affirmation echoed the truth of my dream. Yet one conversation stood apart.

A woman approached my pastor, winded, almost like she had been running. He waved me over. With urgency in her eyes, she told me her story.

She explained that when she arrived that morning, she sat near my wife, whom she recognized from a life group. She glanced at me and thought, "Maybe that is Michelle's husband." Then, suddenly, everything went numb. She had to excuse herself to the restroom and splash water on her face.

When the service started, she sat back down. But when I stepped on stage to read my poem, she nearly fainted. She knew she had to speak to me. With my pastor standing beside her, tears in her eyes. she looked at me and said. "I have been told to say."

"It's going to be OK."

Echoes of a Silent Battle

My armor is scarred, battled and beaten.

Damage to my chest, but my heart is still beating.

I'm lost, not defeated.

Forward I move.

Because retreat has no reason.

*The enemy is near, fierce veterans of fear.
kin of sin-
a vow of the end.*

One by one the enemy falls. The screams of failure echo through the halls.

As I watch the enemy lie—I'm confused by its cries.

Forward I move.

Not seeing my demise.

The battle ground is covered in stone.
Caution of failure, deep as bone.

My sword is swift advancing with every blow.

My arrogance is winning.
Only to be controlled by my foe.

Alone I've become.
Pride has stollen my edge.

Many battles fought.
This can't be the end.

The sound of the drums have faded.
And the light is confusing my glance

Forward I move

Is my only chance.

Still frame memories have shadowed the way. I have no direction, so I kneel and pray.

Heavenly Father, forgive me of my arrogance and pride. I know your grace has power beyond my thoughts. I ask you for the strength to recognize the enemy. Lord, help me hear the wisdom and follow your way. I surrender. In Your Name, I pray and believe.

Amen.

Forward we move.

Surrender has become my victory. I was the battle

living in envy.

Saved by grace.

He never gave up on me.

Believing In Christ.

"I has become We."

About the Author

Mario Rios is a husband, father, foreman, and a man who once wrote in silence . After 20 years of keeping his words to himself, he shared a single poem on his 40th birthday that moved hearts and opened doors. This collection is a result of battles fought, faith rediscovered, and the simple act of not giving up. He lives in New Mexico and continues to write-not for himself, but for anyone still walking through there own silent battles.

Discipline Over Motivation

Do not let challenge define your life—define the challenge.
You are not the victim; you are the victor.
Welcome hard things and watch how you grow.
Savor small victories like a last meal.
Receive the gifts of life;
they are only the start of new beginnings.
Structure and purpose require discipline.
Motivation is a choice—but discipline is life.

Every step in this rebirth is a lesson.
Learning how to shape your inner self—the part no one sees.
You can't outrun it. It is there in the quiet nights,
when your eyes are closed. Knowing your secrets,
that inner voice that has made you think
you were not good enough,
when you are.

Each step holds keys to self-awareness.
Expect self-doubt. Welcome it when it knocks.
Leave the door unlocked—it can not enter unless you invite it.

You are the one who challenges the challenge. Use it to feed the
fire you ignited in battle.
This may be the hardest work you ever do.

Pain has weighed on you so long it feels familiar—almost
comfortable.

But the real question is not life itself;
it is how you see life.
See that "bad luck" is the challenge.

Your definition is how you deal with it.
Learning to handle the hard and the complicated becomes the stepping stones to self improvement and salvation.

Good days still slip through the cracks of ordinary time; do not miss them.

Guard your emotions and meet each moment with care, or you will drift into fatigue and start to believe that you have a target on your back.
This is what the enemy wants.

Understand that most days are simply another battle.
Everyday requires your attention.
These are the small victories we savor.

When something happens, do not ignore it. Pause. Pray on it. Think it through. Do not act on that burst of energy in your chest that feeling is an alarm now—your cue to pay attention.

Author's Notes:

Dear Reader,

I never imagined I would one day share my battle with anyone—let alone share it alongside the writings and poems that became my outlet.

If you find yourself deep in these pages, living the battle as you read, please know this: it is about finding peace within. My purpose is simple—to start a conversation. For me, it only took one conversation to begin my healing journey, and that journey continues today. Each day is not perfect, but every day is better than yesterday.

I want to encourage you to talk to someone—whether at church, with a trusted friend, or with a counselor. My pastor was the first person I spoke with, and through his guidance and relationships, I found both the spiritual and professional help I needed.

You are not alone. This is the very reason I write. The fact that you are reading these words is enough to know that He loves you. I am only moving the pencil—these are His words placed on my heart, for you.

Someone is counting on you.

Make one day—day one. This isn't for me.

"It is for you."

.

Made in the USA
Coppell, TX
12 January 2026

68875099R10021